THE MAPLE HOUSE

The True Story of a Haunting

Rebecca Patrick-Howard
Written as Jeanie Dyer

GW00984803

The Maple House

The True Story of a Haunting

"a must read for anyone interested in the paranormal" - Amazon reviewer

Jeanie Dyer

Table of Contents

DISCLAIMER

The following story is true. However, some names and identifying locations have been changed.

FOREWORD

The following story really happened. Names and identifying locations and certain information have been changed for different reasons, some of which might become more understandable as you read on.

My story is not a long one, although it took place over the course of two years. Many of the events, when taken on their own, are not extraordinary in and of themselves.

A lot of people have asked me why we stayed in the house as long as we did. The truth of the matter is, we were never completely sure that there was something paranormal or even unusual going on around us—at least not until the end when we started piecing our experiences together. Although many bad things happened in the Maple House, a lot of *good* things did as well. It wasn't always a time filled with terror or sadness. There was quite a bit of joy within the walls and, for the most part, that canceled out whatever else was going on.

Things began to change, however, and then it became an *un*happy place. When I look back on the house now, I feel a certain amount of dread, tension, and my memories are tinged with darkness. This makes me unbearably sad because we started out so happy there, excited, ready to take on a new adventure. That everything could end so horribly in a place where we'd counted on many of our dreams coming true feels like a cruel joke.

I couldn't tell you when our haunting started. I suppose it really started with the music, although I can think of smaller things that pre-date even that.

I can't even tell you, for sure, that it *was* a haunting. Times have changed attitudes when it comes to hauntings and ghosts and we expect more out of them these days. I know I did. I learned that in reality, unlike in the movies, you don't always get the loud noises, disappearing specters, and levitating objects. It's much more subtle. The downside of this is it makes you more apt to question your sanity and what you're experiencing. By the time you finish reading this you might not even be convinced that there was anything supernatural at play at all; that everything was just a string of unhappy coincidences, random life events strung together one after another. My husband's mother once said life was just a series of events, some good and some bad.

And perhaps that is true. Maybe what happened to us at the Maple House didn't have anything to do with ghosts or negative energy. Everyone goes through tough times. This may have simply been *ours*.

But I know what I felt. And I know what I saw.

Except for the one incident witnessed only by my then three-year-old son, there were no "ghosts": no apparitions, no floating heads, no Hollywood-type "Lady in White" figures roaming up and down our hallways. We didn't catch orbs in our photographs. We didn't invite ghost hunters into our house to catch disembodied voices on EVPs.

But we felt targeted.

At the end, I will let you decide what was going on—if the house and land did, indeed, have something going on inside it or if everything could be chalked up to coincidence and the randomness that the Universe often presents.

There will be no clear resolution to this story. No happy ending. No smoking gun. For awhile I searched for answers. I tried to research the history of the area (the house itself was not old), tried to glean insightful information that might explain what was going on. I became obsessed with the *understanding* of the events. If you walk away from this feeling frustrated, unsettled, or without resolution you must know that I feel the same way. There were never any answers, only speculation.

For almost two years I felt as though something might be after my family, especially my children. I honestly wondered if we would all make it out alive. And, unfortunately, one of us didn't. By the end, I was holding onto my family so tightly that the sheer panic was overwhelming and strangling. The terror that something *more* would happen to us was a blanket that enveloped me and kept me suffocated, unable to breathe. And then we left. There are times, though, especially late at night when I'm sitting up all alone and I feel as though whatever "it" was that haunted us is still there, waiting.

THE MAPLE HOUSE

For years I've had this recurring dream: I am living in a haunted house but nobody will believe it's haunted. The ghosts are after me, night after night. They're attacking me, trying to kill me. They chase me and suffocate me and try to get inside of me. I beg everyone in the house to leave, to move, but they laugh at me. The dream always ends with me screaming, pleading, and crying. I wake up covered in sweat, my heart pounding.

Our time at the Maple House didn't start out frightening. Indeed, it began as a dream home. It's a funny thing about hauntings, though: They're not always scary. Sometimes you even find yourself hoping that something else will happen.

6

In the beginning, at least, a lot of *good* things happened to us in the house. We loved it there. The strange things that occurred, the "bad luck" we seemed to encounter, was intermixed with a lot of joy. It was easy to ignore the rest at first. Life isn't like a Hollywood horror movie, where every moment is filled with terror and dread. The dread, I learned, builds slowly. It eats away at you a little bit over time, like a sickness, until it consumes you and fills you. You start questioning everything you do and feel.

On more than one occasion I thought I might be going crazy. Sometimes, I still feel like I *am*.

We weren't necessarily looking to move. My husband Pete and our two-year-old son Sam and I were moderately happy in our brick ranch-style house in the country. Pete and I were a little concerned that it was so close to the road but Sam was a good child and listened most of the time. We were renting the house and had made it ours as best we could. I had a decent job, although it was stressful, and Pete had a great job, although it didn't pay much. We were probably what most people would consider "to be middle class", if a little on the lower end. We lived paycheck to paycheck like everyone else in the area and dreamed of a day when we wouldn't.

We were happy, but we were also restless. After several years of struggling financially we felt like we should have been doing better at that point in our marriage. Most nights, after Sam fell asleep, we'd stay awake and sit on the couch, Pete rubbing my feet, while we'd talk about what we wanted to do next, where we wanted to go, what we saw ourselves *really* doing.

"I'm stressed," I'd moan as Pete flipped through the TV channels, looking for something to watch. Cable, thee basic package, was one of our few indulgences. That and name brand ice cream. "Work stinks. I don't want to go in tomorrow."

"You say that every day," he'd remind me and we'd go back to watching "Criminal Minds" or "The Golden Girls." The conversation would be over because it didn't have anywhere else to go.

I wasn't in the career I wanted to be in. I did what I did because it was a job, but as a public servant in the child welfare sector there were many rough days. I couldn't leave my duties at the office and often worked late and on weekends. I was on call 24/7. I was around so much neglect, sadness, and suffering that the lining in my stomach was being eaten away from stress. I cried a lot. More and more I found myself struggling to get out of bed in the morning, on the verge of tears at the thought of another day in my office or getting a new client.

I loved the children I worked with and enjoyed many of their parents but I still wasn't happy; I knew it wasn't my "calling." The stress of work was causing stress in our marriage and I was sorry for that, too. I wanted more free time to garden, to play with Sam, to hang out with Pete and relax and not have to keep my phone on me at all times with constant text messages from my supervisor interrupting us.

That previous winter we'd had a terrible ice storm, one of the worst ones on record. When our power went out in the middle of the storm while Pete was at work teaching a night class I'd bundled Sam up and stuck him in the car. We'd driven to my mother's, thinking the storm was over. It wasn't. What would eventually become eleven inches of ice pounded the car as I tried to get to my mother's house in another county. Her road was a deathtrap; as I moved inch by inch down the narrow lane the trees crashed around me and I spun off the road into a ditch, nearly tumbling into the river. A neighbor had to come and get us because the falling trees crushed my car and blocked us in. When we finally made it to her house we were wet, cold, crying, and scared. My supervisor had immediately texted me and asked me to drive three counties over to check on a client. At our own home we were without power for three weeks and had to spend that time with my mother at her house. We lost all the food in our refrigerator and freezer and were out nearly $1,000. Our pipes froze and burst. We received no relief, yet I still had to work more than twelve hours a day, using our agency's budget to restock the refrigerators of the families we worked with. It had been a sobering experience.

"I need to find another job," I said to Pete that spring.

He agreed. "Rebecca, you're crying because you don't want to go to work. I never see you and your agency has no consideration for your health. How many times have you been asked to drive in a snowstorm? Work during tornados? Go into homes with highly infectious diseases?"

It was true. I'd brought home scabies, MRSA, head lice more than once, swine flu, and more infections than I could count.

"I'll think of something," I promised. "I swear I'll make it better for us."

And I tried.

In high school and college I'd spent a lot of my time writing books, screenplays, and poetry. I loved writing and tried to do it in what little spare time I had, but lately all I wanted to do was sleep. I was tired, cranky, and almost certainly depressed. I toyed around with the idea of making writing a fulltime career, but had no idea how to proceed with that. I was no Stephen King or Nora Roberts. I'd never even finished writing the novel I'd been working on for several years.

It seemed impossible to try and make a career out of such a thing, but writing made me happy. A lot of my job depended on case notes and extensive report writing, however, and after spending so much time doing it for work I didn't feel like devoting any time to creative writing anymore. Each day, it felt like more pieces of me were floating away and I didn't like it. I didn't want another ten years to go by and suddenly look back on my life and regret not doing the things I loved.

It was time to make a change while I still could.

One afternoon, out of boredom, I began playing around on Craigslist. I liked to look at houses for rent and for sale, just for the fun of it. Like most people, I guess, I dreamed of the day my ship would come in and we could afford to buy a big house with a big yard and live the "dream." I liked to see what all was out there, even if it was just fantasizing about things we could never have. Real estate was my escape in those days and long after Sam went to sleep I'd scour the ads, looking at virtual tours and videos and showing Pete the ones I found. Of course, we couldn't afford anything more than what we were paying but it was fun to imagine. One day, we'd tell ourselves, *one day…*

There was only one house listed for rent in my area that day and I did a double take, thinking it *must* be a mistake. The rent was more than twice what we were currently paying, and we were on the high end of the spectrum for our community. I was intrigued. The ad didn't have a picture, but it boasted more than 4,000 square feet and five bedrooms.

"Hey Pete!" I hollered from the office. "You gotta come listen to this!"

I read him the description aloud while he swung little Sam around by the waist and tried to entertain him.

"Huh," he said when I was finished. "Sounds nice I guess."

"'Nice'?" I shook my head. "It sounds *great*!"

Considering the cost of the rent, he was less than enthused.

To be honest, I didn't know of many houses in my county that could even fit that description. It was a small place, the county seat having fewer than 3,000 residents. While not everyone knew everyone, big houses did not go unnoticed. And, for our neck of the woods, 4,000 square feet was a *big* house. In fact, it was almost a mansion.

My mother was coming over that afternoon for a visit and I showed the ad to her. She was much more enthusiastic.

"Wanna go see it?" she asked with excitement.

"Heck yeah!" I cried, grabbing my shoes. Sam stretched his chubby little arms upwards, asking to go along. We were a team, the two of us, so I scooped him up and took him along with us.

Always up for an adventure, we decided to go for a drive and check it out. "We're not moving," my husband hollered as we sailed out the door. He hated moving more than anything in the world.

"I *know*!" I yelled back. "We just want to see what it looks like! We're just bored!"

He rolled his eyes and shooed us on, shaking his head in disbelief. He couldn't understand why we might want to get our hopes up about something that was so far out of our reach.

The address was in a part of the county we weren't familiar with and the house was isolated, even more remote than my own country home.

From its position high on a mountaintop we could see it nearly a mile before we reached it and then a gravel road took us nearly straight up to the top. "No wonder we didn't know anything about it," my mom said as we bounced up the rocky road. "You can't see it from the road and it's pretty set back. Hate to drive up this in the winter." (That was, by the way, my mom's standby remark any time we looked at a house with a hill or narrow road.)

Oh, but it was beautiful, though. The high price tag was immediately obvious.

"Damn," I couldn't help but say as I stared in awe. "This is *nice*! I've always wanted to live in a mini-mansion."

It looked like something out of a fairy tale. With its dark brown wooded-sides, tall rose bushes flanking the wraparound porch, apple trees nearly reaching both the second-floor balconies, and mountains rising up on all three sides it appeared to be growing from the very ground it was built upon. There was an organic look to the house, as though it had emerged from the land rather than having been built *on* it.

It didn't look very old; maybe thirty years at most. From the driveway we had a panorama view of the valley below as the mountains stretched out before us.

It was late afternoon so the sun had dropped down in the sky and cast a golden shadow over everything. The valley below us appeared to be on fire, the mountains a purple haze in the background. Maple trees shaded the front and from that point onwards we would refer to it as "The Maple House." A back deck led to a wooden jungle gym with a slide, swings, and little club house and there was even a small barn and pasture. The rest of the backyard was surrounded by thick, dark woods.

Sam couldn't contain his excitement. "Can we live here?" he shouted from the backseat. "Can I play on the slide?"

"You want to look at it?" Mom asked. She tried to act casual but I could see the eagerness in her eyes. She was just itching to get out and look around.

"Well, we're here," I shrugged, also trying to act like I wasn't nearly as impressed as I was. "Why not?"

So, we called the number in the ad and within half an hour the caretaker arrived and was letting us in. He was the owner's brother-in-law and apparently oversaw the house while the owner lived and worked out of state.

"There's not a chance he'll come back within the next few months and want his house back is there?" I asked, a little worried. I don't know why I cared. It's not like we were actually thinking about *renting* it.

"No," George, an older gentleman with an easygoing manner laughed. "He's been gone for almost fifteen years. He probably won't come back until he retires and that's a long time off!"

If it was possible, the house looked even better on the inside. The kitchen was massive, nearly the size of the small farmhouse Pete and I had rented when we first got married. It had everything a couple on "House Hunters" would want: granite countertops, stainless steel appliances, new cabinets...There were two separate bars in the kitchen, one with stools to make it a dine-in, but there was also a formal dining room as well with a glass chandelier.

Two small parlors, a master bedroom with ensuite bath, half bath, and a large living room with cathedral ceilings made up the downstairs. The upstairs had four bedrooms, two full baths, and a very large family room with a pool table. Two of the upstairs bedrooms had doors that opened out onto the balconies we'd seen from outside. The master bedroom downstairs also had its own private outside seating area.

It was easily one of the most beautiful places I had ever seen. Without realizing it, I mentally began placing our furniture throughout the rooms and started decorating it before we even made it back outside.

"Which room do I get, Mommy?" Sam asked.

"Shhh," I hissed. "We'll talk about it later. We're NOT renting it! We're just looking. Looking with Nana."

We thanked George and drove back to my house in silence. When Mom finally turned off the engine I looked at her and said, "Well, *I* liked it."

Before the night was over, one of us had made the suggestion that we all move in together and share the expenses. I don't know who came up with the idea first, but it seemed like a good one at the time.

"We could do it," Mom said quite seriously. "We'd have plenty of room there for all of us..."

My mother was also renting and wasn't completely satisfied with her house. It was a nice place, but it was located on the river and its proximity to the dark, muddy water made her nervous. (With good reason, as it turned out. Months after she moved the whole downstairs of her former house flooded.)

She made good money herself and could have afforded the Maple House on her own. There's no way we could have, of course. If we moved in together, however, we could help her with the bills and take some of the strain off and it wouldn't be that much more than what we were currently paying.

"You all could take the upstairs and I'd have the downstairs," she suggested. "And then we'd share the kitchen."

I knew that meant I'd still do most of the cooking, Mom's idea of making dinner is to call for reservations, but it sounded like it could work.

It took a little more to convince Pete.

"Do we really want to move?" he asked. "Were we even talking about moving? Why would we do this?"

"No," I answered, "we weren't talking about moving. But we felt like a change and this might be good for us. It's a beautiful house and Sam would love it there. The whole upstairs, which we'd have, is bigger than what we've got right now. I've never lived in a place like that before. And it'd even be cheaper since we'd be sharing bills with Mom. Maybe I could quit my job and freelance fulltime. I could finish my book and supplement through copywriting."

Over the past few months I'd been taking on more and more freelancing jobs, mostly writing content for people's blogs and newsletters. While they'd only supplied me with some extra spending money so far, with more time on my hands and real dedication to the work there was a possibility of it becoming more like an actual career. I'd been thinking about that a lot over the past few weeks.

"The summer's coming up and your job slows down. If we *were* going to move, this would be the best time to do it," I added.

It was May.

Eventually, we all came to the decision to just do it. Sam was ecstatic. Pete wasn't. "I hate moving," he grumbled. "We ought to just throw everything away and start from scratch."

But we did it. The move was long and hard and it was more difficult saying goodbye to our little ranch house than I thought it was going to be. We'd had some good times there and it was a cozy place, warm and inviting. It wasn't the mini mansion the Maple House was, but it was the place where Sam learned to walk, where I experimented with recipes, where Sam and I had danced in the kitchen every night to my old record player, and where we'd talked about our dreams.

The first night at the Maple House, the three of us slept on a mattress in what would eventually be our office/guest room upstairs since that was the only room that had any furniture in it. It was a restless night since we were getting used to a new place, but we were excited.

GETTING SETTLED

Over the course of the next few weeks, we did our best to get moved, unpack, and settle in. Pete wasn't anyone to let grass grow under his feet once he got into a new place. He wanted to be settled *right* away. Within days he had most of our part of the house unpacked and organized. It already felt lived in and comfortable.

I bought bulbs and flowers and seeds and got to work on the outside. I dug up old beds and turned things over and planted like the dickens. Sam drove his little cars around, chased the cats, and played on the jungle gym. The downstairs was so big that he took to putting toys in his little shopping cart and pushing it around so that he could easily transport them from one room to another.

I, myself, would forget just how big the house really was until I wanted a drink in the middle of the night and was in the office and had to first walk down one hall, then down the long steep flight of stairs, and then down the other long hall on the bottom floor. It literally took almost three whole minutes. Sometimes, I'd get down to the kitchen and forget what I was there for.

Sam did thrive in his new surroundings. He was a happy child anyway, always giggling and smiling and ready to tell his little jokes. He was the light of all our lives. Up there on the mountaintop, he seemed to come alive even more. There, he could run around in the yard without being watched as closely. He collected rocks and picked wildflowers for me, we went for walks in the woods and picked out places we might like to set up our tents and camp in, and at night we sat on our front porch swing and watched the stars as we rocked back and forth and talked about all the good times to come there.

I quit my job as a family therapist and began freelancing fulltime as planned. Pete would take Sam to preschool in the mornings and I would work during the nights and sleep in until about noon. I worked better at night with everyone asleep and with Sam gone during the day I could sleep in. It was much easier finding work and clients when I didn't have my other job limiting my time and I soon had my hands full.

I noticed a difference in our family life almost immediately. I was more relaxed and happier. In the evenings we'd rent movies and watch them together on the couch in the living room or lounge on the sofa in the family room, playing board games. I started experimenting with new recipes and took my time cooking meals now that I didn't feel as rushed. Sam would help me, dragging his little stool up to the counter and helping me stir batter and soups and season vegetables.

We'd been in the house for about a month when Pete returned home one morning, upset. I heard him stomping around downstairs when he should have been at work and I went down to make sure everything was okay.

"My car died," he muttered. "Just stopped in the middle of our road. Your mom gave me a ride back."

"What do you think happened?" I asked. It was an old Dodge Dynasty, but it had served us well for a long time as a second vehicle. Frankly, I was surprised it had lasted as long as it did.

He shrugged. "I don't know. I guess I need to call a tow truck or get back over there and try to get it home. I pulled it over onto someone's grass so I need to do something soon."

He went back about an hour later, but the car was gone. The property owners had called a wrecker themselves and our car was hauled to a salvage yard. "So much for people being friendlier in the country," I grumbled.

The salvage yard was so far out of town that it would have cost us nearly $100 to have it towed to a mechanic, not to mention the $100 it was going to take to get it out. In the end, the guy paid us $50 to let him scrap it. I cried a little, saying goodbye to it. I'm sentimental that way.

Losing the Dodge put us down to one vehicle which meant I didn't have one when he left for work every day. We couldn't afford to buy another one, especially since I was still making payments on mine. I rarely left the house during the day anyway, but I liked having the option of being able to leave.

"It's okay," I said. "I don't need to get out and go anywhere. When we get our tax refund we'll find something cheap and get another one." I tried not to think about the fact that it was only June and that was almost seven months away.

Two months later, my mother's car also stalled on our road and this left *her* without a vehicle. She ended up taking Sam to preschool, Pete to work, and then herself to work. Organizing the schedules was a little bit like a brain teaser. It was not a good summer for our cars and we cursed our bad luck.

"Oh well," I sighed after Mom's quit. "It could be worse, I guess."

We had no idea.

The Music

I can't remember when the music started. I've tried and tried to piece it together in my mind, but those early weeks and months blend together. All in all, we only lived in the Maple House for two years. I should remember everything that happened right down to the week, or at least the month. But things get blurry after awhile. That's especially true after people started dying.

The music was the first real scare, though. That's when I started paying attention. The cars were annoying; the music made me sit up and listen.

I never played music at night. I never left the television on. I don't like having too much distraction going while I'm writing. Occasionally, I'll let music play during the daytime but I get really involved in the music and on more than one occasion I've actually started typing the lyrics instead of the sentence I'm meant to be writing. That's generally *not* a good thing.

So the first time I heard the soft, low melody I assumed it was my mother downstairs. Maybe she had the radio on or maybe she was underneath me, watching television. She got up to use the bathroom a lot during the night and she often had trouble going back to sleep so it wasn't implausible to think she might have popped in a movie or something.

My office

I don't know how many nights I listened to the sounds before they truly registered with me. They were just *there,*

fading in with the rest of the noises one has to get used to when moving into a new place.

One night, however, I realized that the voices floating in and out of my consciousness were not in English. They were low, rhythmic, almost chanting. The musicality was not something I would have called modern. A slow and steady drumbeat accompanied the voices and intermittently I'd hear a flute or a wind instrument I couldn't put my finger on. Sometimes, it would be quick and up-tempo. Other times, it would be soft and sad, even melancholy, and I'd stop typing and sit back and listen, straining my ears to try and catch the words. They were always just a little bit out of my grasp, however–so close to me and yet just out of reach.

It became a game to wrap my mind around what I was hearing. I'd patiently and wait and listen for the music, straining my ears and mind to latch onto the noises. When they'd begin I'd stop typing, hold my breath, and steady my heartbeat, feeling like the slightest movement on my end would make it all go away. I was becoming obsessed with the strange sounds, intent on determining their source and what they meant.

One evening, I became so wrapped up in the gentle, somber tones that despite the chills that raced up my arms my eyes filled with tears and I cried as though I missed something I couldn't even put my finger on. There was an aching in my heart that made it hurt, a gentle ache that wasn't even that unwelcomed.

It was at that point I got up and went down the stairs, fully expecting to see my mom sitting in front of the television set or listening to a recording I didn't know we had.

The living room was empty.

As I lightly knocked on her bedroom door and then opened it, I saw that she was sitting up in bed, turned to her window. The moonlight fell across her figure and she wasn't moving. She stayed as still as a stone, her head cocked at angle.

She was listening as well.

"You hear that?" she whispered without looking in my direction.

I crept toward the middle of the room and gently climbed up on the bed with her.

"The music?" I whispered back. "I thought that was you."

"And I thought it was *you*," she said.

"Is this the first time you've heard it?"

"No, I've been hearing it a long time. I just assumed you were upstairs listening to the radio."

"I don't have anything on up there," I explained.

"That's not all I've heard," my mom said, continuing to keep her voice soft. "One night I heard you and Pete upstairs on your balcony, talking. I could almost make out what you were saying."

Now *this* really startled me and I could feel the chills returning and popping up on the back of my neck. I had only been on our balcony once, and that was the day we moved in. On that particular occasion, we'd seen a rather large hornet's nest. I had informed Pete that I would not be going back out there until he removed it. I didn't do hornets.

"Uh, that wasn't us," I said.

"But I *heard* you," she insisted.

"Mom, I've been working. Pete goes to bed way before me. I don't go until daylight." I was frustrated that this didn't seem to have an easy explanation and Mom was still convinced that it was us making the noise and not realizing it.

Not ones to let anything go, we decided to investigate. She got up and the two of us took a little walk through the house. The music was weak, but still faintly audible. "Maybe it's echoing down from the valley," I said. "We *are* up on a mountain."

So, we opened the front door and stepped outside. It was quiet, save for a few crickets and frogs. We stood there for a moment, neither one of us speaking, and listened. It was peaceful there on the porch, what with the night symphony going on around us. It felt oddly comforting knowing that we were surrounded by the sounds nature made each night. But our song wasn't there. It wasn't outside.

The minute we closed the door, however, and were back inside the house the music started up again. It was *in* the house.

"I don't know," Mom sighed at last, dropping to the couch in frustration. "At least it's pretty."

Having had experiences with the paranormal in the past, however, I was concerned. The music *was* pretty, but it was unsettling. I'd never heard anything so plainly before, at least not for such an extended period of time–at least something that wasn't meant to be there.

I'd heard fleeting sounds, sounds that rushed by quickly and were over with almost as soon as they started, but this lingered. It was different, intentional. I felt like it *wanted* to be heard.

This unnerved me.

At times I would sit in my office chair, pillows underneath me to raise me up to the desktop, and stare into the darkness off my balcony. I'd listen to the reverberations to try and expound them in some way.

What did they mean? Why were we hearing them? Were they just leftover energy the house or land was remembering? Was there really a ghostly band somewhere, keeping up with a beat it couldn't forget?

Pete, who was always asleep when the music played, was untouched by this phenomena. He'd never had a paranormal experience and while he believed us, he wasn't helpful. I couldn't talk to him about what was going on because he simply had no frame of reference for it. I tried to wake him up on many occasions to get him to listen but Pete was an incredibly sound sleeper. Even after waking up it took him at least half an hour to become lucid. By the time I roused him and got him awake enough to be coherent the music was always gone. On the occasions he tried to stay up and listen for it himself, it never came.

Jim

The house, with its isolation and decks and porches and large kitchen and dining areas was perfect for parties and entertaining. And entertain we did.

It was possible to play our music at any level we wanted, sing, and carry on into the wee hours of the morning without any neighbors complaining because, well, there really *weren't* any neighbors to complain. We had two big parties that summer and the second one that celebrated the end of the season was one many of us will never forget.

The first party was all about the food and introducing people to the house. We were excited to have our friends, Ashley and Jim, over. Jim was particularly enamored of the house and the scenery at first and couldn't say enough about how beautiful it was.

"If you want another roommate, you know who to call," he kidded as he walked through the rooms, opening doors and peeking into all the cabinets.

"Seriously," I agreed. "Can you believe *we* live in a place like this? And I don't even feel like I have a real job half the time. This must be how rich people feel!"

I was trying to spend more time working on my fiction. I was attempting to learn better time management skills, too. It was hard, because I would do anything to procrastinate, but I wanted to finish some of the novels I'd started years ago. Money was tight but we were happy and I was being more productive than I'd ever been as far as my writing was concerned. I truly felt like if I could see something through and really make a commitment then we might be on the right track to something great.

Jim had a lively, fun personality and had been one of our best family friends for almost twenty years. I considered him one of my partners in crime and he always came to our get-togethers, along with Ashley, and prepared the best food. In fact, when I graduated from college they'd even catered the entire the meal themselves for my graduation party as a gift to me and he'd made my wedding bouquet. We loved exploring old houses together, sometimes crawling through windows to take pictures of abandoned fireplace mantles, winding staircases forgotten by others, and beautiful hardwood floors suffering from neglect. Few people understood my love for exploring or my passion for history like Jim.

Jim was in good spirits that day at the Maple House, making his rounds and visiting with everyone in the house. He was full of energy and laughter, running from one room to the next with excitement as he opened closet doors, peeked into cupboards, and gazed at our fabulous view.

"I could sit here on the porch all day long," he sighed at one point as we looked at the mountains together. The sun was starting to set and we were on our fourth glass of wine. I was feeling loose and relaxed, content with the pleasant company and good food we had spread out in the kitchen. It was one of those perfect summer evenings that felt like nothing bad could ever truly happen.

"It has to be the best view in the county doesn't it?" I agreed.

He nodded. "But..."

"But what?" I could sense he had something on his mind, but was hesitant to continue. That wasn't like Jim. If anything, he put his foot in his mouth more often than not. He certainly wasn't one to hold back. I was surprised, too. All evening he'd gushed about how much he loved the house, complimenting everything from the bathrooms to the back deck. His hesitation now concerned me.

"Have you felt or seen anything here Rebecca?" It came out all in a rush, like he was embarrassed to even mention it. His ears even turned a slight shade of pink.

"You mean like a ghost?" I laughed. "No. I haven't seen or felt anything. Just had bad luck with the cars. And heard some music at night. But we're not real sure where that's coming from. Could be from down in the valley somewhere."

"Could be," he agreed but didn't look convinced. He looked troubled. "But I doubt it. Too many trees. They'd block the sound."

"Why James, do you think our house is haunted?" I teased him. "You think every place is haunted!"

It was true and he knew it. James loved a good ghost story and where there wasn't one he'd make one up. This time, though, he rolled his eyes and lit up a cigarette. "Well, most places probably *do* have a ghost or two around. I feel something different here, though. Something pulling at me. I can't explain it. Maybe it's nothing. Just forget about it," he shrugged it off and smiled then, looking more like himself.

But I could tell he was still unsettled and troubled. I tried not to let it bother me for the rest of the evening but I'd known him long enough to know that he took these things seriously and if something hadn't truly been bothering him he'd at least been joking about it with me.

Jim and Ashley weren't able to attend the second party, the last one of summer, but we saw him two days before when they stopped by to visit. He looked tired, but good. We didn't have the chance to talk much, but I figured I'd call him in a day or two and catch up with him. Again, we walked through the house together and chatted.

"Are you happy here?" he asked, putting his hand on my shoulder. The gravity of his tone disturbed me. I could count on one hand the number of times he'd looked troubled or concerned during our friendship. Something was definitely bothering him and I wanted to get to the bottom of it.

"I really am," I answered honestly. "It's so beautiful and Sam just thrives here. He can play outside and we don't have to worry about the road. There's plenty of space to spread out in. And the pool room is great. We spend most of our time in there. Of course, I get to do a lot more writing and that helps."

"Just be careful, Becky," he said. I smiled. He was one of the few people who could get away with calling me that.

"I will," I promised her but I didn't know what he was worried about. The music disturbed me but it didn't scare me. In fact, I looked forward to it in some strange, macabre one.

"I know I said it before, but there's something here I don't like. It's not the house, it's great," he rushed, "but there's a...tug. Protect yourself if you can. Use sage. Light some candles. But watch your back."

"Oh Jim," I laughed. "We'll be fine!"

There were about thirty other guests at the last party. It was an epic event. Some people even brought tents and camped out. There was drinking, music being played, enough food to fill a banquet hall, Tarot cards, and karaoke.

It went on for hours and hours. I think I might have even napped, woken up, and started over again at one point. One of my friends was married to a guy in a band and his band played a biker rally that night. They came to our house at 2:00 am for the after party and we were still going strong.

It was one of the best nights I believe I've ever had. My last memory of the event was sitting on my deck in the early morning hours with a friend of mine singing John Prine's "Paradise" and nibbling on a spicy chicken leg.

The next thing I remember, my mom was waking me up in bed, telling me that Jim had passed away from a heart attack. He was fifty-five.

FALL AT THE MAPLE HOUSE

That fall was one of the last good, innocent times
we had in our family. It would be the last time in our
collective lives that we would be able to live naïvely,
believing things always turned out well. Jim's death was a
sore spot, and hurt me more than I could have imagined,
but life had to go on and we let it.

We did the usual things we tended to do in the fall:
visited the pumpkin patches, went trick-or-treating, carved
jack-o-lanterns, went to as many fall festivals as
possible...And we met friends for trips to the movies,
nights out to hear local bands play, and dinner. We were
very social back then, hardly sitting still for a minute.

Things were going well for us.

And yet, I was afraid.

The music during the night had stopped. I'd come to
enjoy the music, depend on it. It didn't frighten me or
upset me. I could explain it away as being leftover energy at
worst, as an echo from the valley at the best. Those night
sounds had been tolerable. But what was going on during
the day was inexplicable.

It started with the blast from downstairs. I was
upstairs alone in the early afternoon, working in the
quietness of the house, when all of a sudden I heard a loud

crash from down below. The sound was so loud I thought the china cabinet or something like it had fallen over. The walls even shook a little, their vibration knocking a picture off the wall in the office and sending it to the carpet with a quiet "thud."

Startled, I jumped up and flew down the stairs to see what could possibly have made such a racket, but nothing was out of place. Nobody was there and all the doors were closed and locked.

It was only as I trudged back up the steep staircase that it dawned on me that I could be at risk being there alone during the day. What if the noise had been someone breaking a window, coming in on me? Or someone with a gun? I hadn't been afraid in the house in the daylight hours before, but the noise unnerved me.

What would I *do* if someone came in on me? I talked to Pete about buying a gun. I started keeping a baseball bat in the office with me in the meantime. I didn't want to become crazy paranoid, but I didn't want to be defenseless, either.

View from one of the balconies

A few days later, I was upstairs again, working, when I heard another sound. This time, the clatter was the unmistakable sound of the front door swinging open and hitting the wall behind it. It was a noise I heard every day as Sam ran in and out of the house, forgetting to take care with it. We didn't have a house phone and my cell wasn't charged, but I didn't let that stop me. Feeling like a sitting duck upstairs without any kind of escape route, I picked it up and carried it down the stairs with me, pretending to be on it as I carried on with an imaginary one-sided conversation.

I wasn't very far down the staircase when I saw that the front door, indeed, was standing wide open. A red wasp drifted in, took a look around, and then sailed back out.

43

The sunlight poured in through the opening, peppering the carpet with dashes of light. Through the door, I could see our porch swing rocking gently back and forth in an indistinguishable breeze.

Logic told me it could have been the wind that pushed it open. I didn't want to overreact. Still, I didn't want to *under*react, either. Not having a weapon of any kind in the house, other than the bat which I'd forgotten upstairs, I went to the fireplace and picked up the poker. I quietly shut the front door and locked it and then slowly made my way through the living room, my mother's rooms, the parlor, and dining room.

I yielded the poker high in the air with trembling hands, uncertain how I'd react if someone jumped out at me. It crossed my mind to run out the door, but where would I go? We didn't have any neighbors. I didn't have a car to hop in and drive away.

Again, nothing appeared out of place. I started to laugh at myself for feeling so foolish and nearly put the poker down. When I walked into the kitchen, however, the poker fell to the floor and my cell wasn't far behind it. Every bottom cabinet door was standing wide open.

From that day onwards, I began documenting many of the unexplainable incidents on Facebook. With a cell phone signal that was sporadic, Facebook was my link to the outside world during the day when I was home alone. I could keep the messenger up and feel connected with friends and family, people who were only a few seconds away in the virtual world when the rest of the world felt miles away in reality. The online world became my refuge and I was able to chat with my friends, fill them in on what was happening, and write journal entries regarding what was going on in the house. These things kept me feeling sane.

That wouldn't be the last time my door flew open or strange noises would come from downstairs and when something happened, I could reach out to my friends online.

October 8, 2009

Something is seriously going on in my house. Doors are slamming, the house is shaking, and lights are coming on-yet I'm the only one home. Here I am, walking around with a 3-hole punch and a pair of scissors as weapon, trying to investigate all 15 rooms. And, of course, my phone is in the car somewhere with Mom.

Like · Comment · Promote · Share   14

Not everything happened when I was home by myself, although (in the beginning at least) a lot happened when it felt like only I could see or hear it.

One afternoon, while everyone was home, I was in the pool room upstairs. Lying on the couch with the door closed, I watched something silly on television and tried to recuperate from a headache. Suddenly, a noise at the door distracted me. It was a small scratching sound and I immediately thought it might be Sam, trying to get in. Sometimes he had trouble with the knob.

"Sam?" I asked, grunting as I got to me feet. "Is that you?"

Before I could stand up and get to the door, however, the knob slowly started turning on its own and then, with a "whoosh," the door itself flew open and smacked into the wall behind it.

Nobody was there.

Having no idea what I would find, I walked to the hallway and looked down it. Of course, it was empty. Noises from outside had me glancing out the window where I could see Sam, Pete, and Mom all out in the backyard. I was in the house alone.

My friend Justice, a one-time ghost hunter, suggested
that I set up a video camera in that room in particular
during the night and try to catch something. She herself
had spent the night in my house and had felt something a
little "off." "Turn on the camera before you go to bed or
while you're working, and see what you can get," she
suggested. "It might take a couple of nights but you'll
probably pick something up sooner or later."

Those I talked to did not act as though they thought I
might be crazy. In fact, most people didn't seem that
surprised. Other people besides James had mentioned it,
too, but couldn't put their fingers on it. "I don't know what
I would call it, Rebecca, but there's something watching
you when you're in that house," one friend said. "And I
can't figure out if it's good or bad. But I don't like it."

48

So, I set up the video camera. I let it record for four nights. It didn't record anything unusual. I put it away after that, frustrated and feeling silly. Maybe I really WAS going out of my mind after all.

In addition to the noises, annoying health problems began cropping up for me. Terrible headaches plagued me and no matter how much Excedrin Migraine I popped, or how many naps I tried to take during the afternoon in dark, cool rooms before everyone came home I just couldn't shake them. Some days, the pain was so bad it made it hard to sit up in front of the computer. Every little sound irritated me and I felt as though I suffered from constant motion sickness.

I felt like I was endlessly getting sick, too. From stomach viruses to sinus infections and 24-hour colds it was always something. I bought multi-vitamins and fresh fruits and vegetables just couldn't seem to stay healthy. As soon as one issue cleared up, another one would take its place.

"Maybe there's some negative energy in our house," I said to Pete one night as I turned in early. I wasn't staying up working late at night every night as I had been in the beginning. I missed going to bed at the same time as the rest of my family and as the fall wore on I just seemed to need more rest. "Remember what George said about the family who lived here before us? She was thirty and started coming down with symptoms all of a sudden from out of the blue and within a month was getting diagnosed with MS."

It had startled me at the time to hear about that. The family of five who'd rented the house before us had been professionals, the mother a nurse and the father a professor. She's been healthy by all accounts with no previous health issues. And then, **wham**! The multiple sclerosis diagnosis after just a month of issues. Now we'd heard that she could barely get around and was bound to a wheelchair. They'd moved in with her mother to get extra help with the children. She'd had to quit her job.

"Where would it have come from?" he asked. "The bad energy if it's here?"

It was a fair question. The house wasn't *that* old, we were objectively positive people, and as far as we knew there hadn't been any deaths in it.

"I don't know. We have a lot of old furniture in here. Maybe we brought something in. Or maybe we brought something with us from one of our trips to Europe or an old cemetery or an old house or something. Maybe it just found *us*. But I could do a cleansing…"

Pete smiled. "If it would make you feel better, do what you think you need to do."

Sam and I had planted some white sage back in the summer so I went outside and cut some. Within a few days it was dry enough for me to burn and I went from room to room, letting the smoke drift into all the corners.

I wasn't a religious person so I didn't exactly pray as I did it, but I did ask for all negative energy and evil spirits to be gone. Sam watched me in fascination and I let him wave the bundle around a few times himself, telling him it was "good luck." If nothing else, it boosted my morale and I knew that Jim would have approved. He'd asked me to do it months ago.

Jim had been on my mind a lot over the past few days anyway and another thought struck me. He'd felt something in the house as well. He couldn't articulate it to me, but would it be possible for him to communicate with me *now*?

I waited until everyone was out of the house the next afternoon and walked around upstairs, talking to the air. "Jim," I said softly. (I felt foolish, even though nobody could hear me.) "Are you there?"

From room to room I went, saying his name and talking about how much I missed him and how much I'd like to be able to talk to him and see him again. A few times I even thought I caught something out of the corner of my eye, but when I turned around it was gone.

After about thirty minutes, I gave up. My attempts at communicating with spirits were not very successful.

That night, however, I sat down in the floor of our office with his funeral program, a couple of candles, and a crystal. Sam was asleep and Pete was watching television in the pool room, so I was all alone. It was a warm night so we had the heat off. No fans were running. His funeral program lay beside my leg, flat on the ground.

Closing my eyes, I meditated for a moment and brought James' face to mind. I thought about his laughter, his sense of humor, and the good times we'd shared. I also thought about how sorry I was we didn't get to talk the last time I'd seen him. Suddenly, a warm breeze glided across my knee. Tingles ran up my leg and back and down my arms. I no longer felt alone in the room. There was definitely something else there, something very close. When I opened my eyes, the candle flames were flickering wildly, shooting up into the air and waving about in their containers. I watched them for a moment, focusing on their light, and then to my surprise Jim's funeral program stood straight up, waved back and forth a couple of times, and then gently fell back down to the floor. I was so grateful I cried.

For a fleeting second I had no doubt Jim was in the room with me.

SWEET BABY JAMES

Life went on and although the bumps in the night, and those in the afternoon, continued it wasn't enough to make anyone constantly fearful. It certainly didn't make us want to move.

Pete, for instance, never felt or saw anything at all. My mom eventually made peace with what she'd heard. She'd kind of liked the music and wasn't bothered by it. So far, nobody else had experienced anything they perceived to be negative.

I was the only one who felt uneasy.

Little things happened, but they were explainable. The excruciating headaches, for instance, that couldn't be controlled with any kind of medication were a mystery. Still, we passed them off as migraines or allergic reactions to something. "Maybe I'm allergic to the paint or something," I offered. I ended up taking a lot of naps.

My neurologist was perplexed. A new MRI didn't show anything. "There could be mold in the house," I suggested again. "That might do it."

Sometimes, one of us would lay something down in a room upstairs, only to walk downstairs and find it there minutes later.

We chalked that up to forgetfulness.

We did seem to be experiencing a stream of bad luck, but didn't everyone? For instance, our cat had a litter of kittens and one of them ended up with a warble, or a large worm, in its neck. Pete did his best to get it out and doctor it but it died in the middle of the night. He was distraught.

Lots of financial problems plagued us, problems we'd never had in the past. But those things happened to other people, too. We just decided to tighten our belts a little more. We told ourselves things would get better. We just needed to be more frugal.

And then, in November, we found out I was pregnant. It was a little bit of a shock. We laughed about the way we found out; even at the time it was funny. Pete and I were away for the weekend, celebrating our anniversary. We'd stopped at the Dollar General to pick up a few things for the cabin we were renting and, as a lark really, I bought a pregnancy test. Later, we went to a cheap country restaurant. I took the test in the bathroom. I came back to the table with my mouth wide open.

"I can't believe I just took a Dollar Store pregnancy test in a restaurant bathroom," I laughed. "And it's positive. It's like a redneck love song."

It should have been a joyous, happy time. It wasn't. The pregnancy was plagued with problems from the start.

I'd had a few issues with Sam's pregnancy, but nothing serious: hyperemesis, some unexplained pain, and some vasovagal syncope.

With this pregnancy, however, I felt as though I might be fighting for my life.

By Christmas I had lost twenty-three pounds. Diagnosed with hyperemesis, I spent a great deal of the first two trimesters in the hospital. Even the IV meds couldn't stop the vomiting. We stopped hearing from many of our social friends since we weren't able to go out anymore. I was pale, thin, and sickly. My hair fell out, my skin turned yellow, I suffered from a deep depression, and I had all kinds of vitamin deficiencies because of the lack of nutrients. Over the course of the pregnancy I ended up having a subchorionic hematoma, placenta previa, sciatica, and preeclampsia.

When I wasn't in bed, rolling around from a combination of pain and nausea, I was trying to work to raise money for our added expenses. The house became a virtual prison for me since leaving it became almost impossible. I couldn't venture very far from a bathroom and standing for any period of time was impossible. My mom borrowed a wheelchair for me and that helped, but then sitting became an issue. I needed help brushing my hair, getting dressed, and doing even the simplest of things. I cried a lot.

And then, at thirty-six weeks, I had a complete placental abruption with a massive hemorrhage and little James (named after our friend) was born early.

A couple of blood transfusions later and I was feeling a little better. In fact, I couldn't believe how much better some extra blood and not being pregnant anymore helped. Luckily, James seemed to be doing okay. We all thanked our lucky stars that I just happened to be out of town the day the abruption happened, and close to a hospital. Had I been at home, neither one of us would have made it. As it was, we were only a few blocks from the best hospital in the state.

I couldn't stop thinking about that. I'd been sick throughout the entire pregnancy but on that weekend we'd chosen to get away. It was a holiday weekend and I felt guilty for not spending more time with Sam. We'd borrowed a wheelchair and had driven an hour away to watch a parade and eat at a restaurant. Had we not done that, had we been at the Maple House...

The first thing my mother said when she saw me in the delivery room was, "The blood!" It covered my legs and feet. They'd already cut my dress off of me and thrown it away.

James was early, but he was *strong*. He looked good. After such a long pregnancy, I was ready to get my life back. I felt like I'd been a terrible mother to Sam. For almost nine months I hadn't been able to play with him, cook much, or do any of the things he liked to do. And at such a young age, three, he couldn't even remember a time when I wasn't "sick."

We turned one of the bedrooms into James' room, but we also put a cradle in our office so he could sleep in there while one of us was working. We wanted him close.

He was a sweet baby. He rarely fussed, even when he had a full diaper. Sam got used to him very quickly and brought him toys. He wanted to play with him right away and we had to explain to him that he was too little to play the way Sam wanted to.

Our friends hadn't really started to come back around yet, but we were hopeful. I was hurt that so many had disappeared during my pregnancy but I figured maybe it was because they didn't know what to say or do.

In the weeks following James' birth we went on picnics in the backyard, went to the county fair, ate out at local restaurants, went for walks, and tried to start our new life as a larger family. We were finding our groove.

At night, I would sit up with James and work or we'd watch movies together in the family room upstairs. He was a good snuggle bunny and together we went through many new releases like "Brideshead Revisited" and "Valentine's Day."

And then, one early Saturday morning, I got up to go get him dressed, and found he had passed away in his sleep in our office in his cradle.

My baby died at seven weeks old. The cause of death was undetermined.

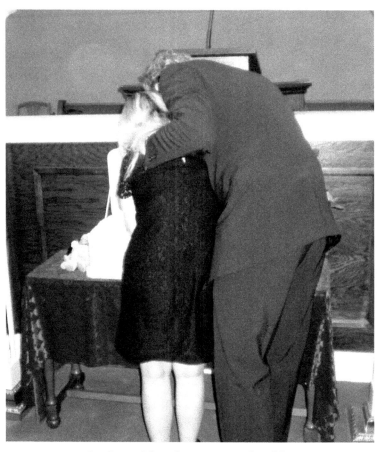

Casket with orb over my shoulder

MORE BAD LUCK

Just four days after burying my son, my father
suffered the first of two heart attacks he'd have that fall.

A week after my father's first heart attack, Mom had a
stroke in her sleep. She lived, but went on to have several
smaller ones that fall.

A week after Mom's stroke, Pete's mother died.

Followed shortly by his grandmother.

And not long after, his grandfather.

And then, one evening, we came home and found both
of Sam's beloved dogs, Yellow and Louie, dead. No
apparent cause of death. They were inside.

In November, almost three months after losing James,
we found out we were pregnant again. We were trying. Two
days later, my husband lost his job.

ANOTHER PREGNANCY

We thought James' pregnancy was hard. It was almost nothing compared to this one. The doctor assured me that what had happened with James' pregnancy was rare and would not likely be repeated. He was wrong. Well, I guess in a way he was right. Some of the things *were* new.

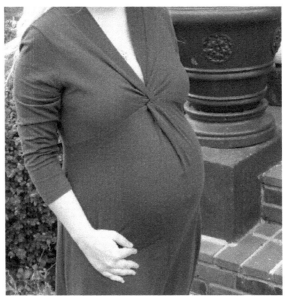

The list of complications was endless: hyperemesis, placenta previa, subchorionic hematoma, intrauterine growth restriction, partial placental abruption, sciatica, gestational diabetes, preeclampsia...

For almost nine months I floated through a sea of depression, grief, and sickness. I no longer felt in control of my thoughts or emotions. The things I'd done to prepare for my other pregnancies were almost impossible. I couldn't go shopping because I couldn't be away from the toilet for more than half an hour at a time. I was weak, unable to stand or sit for any length of time. I'd frequently lose consciousness while vomiting, awakening to find myself in a pool of sickness on the bathroom or bedroom floor. I considered abortion at one point. I considered suicide.

Luckily, I found a support group of other women who were going through something similar and found I wasn't alone in these thoughts and that at least made me feel less crazy.

Our former friends never fully returned. We were alone most of the time, with nothing but our grief, loneliness, and each other to cling to. It was a terrible time of isolation–a time of anger, despondency, and very little hope. We saved what goodness we had for Sam and tried to provide him with the best life we could.

Again, much of that pregnancy was spent in the hospital. At one point they were feeding me sixteen pills a day just to try and stop the vomiting. Potassium, magnesium, and other vitamins were being pumped into me at the same time by IV. The line would blow almost every day, thanks to the amount of medicine that was being shot through it, so my arms were black and blue. Nurses had to help me get to the bathroom, walk up and down the halls, and brush my hair.

When I'd have a moment of relief the head of Obstetrics would send down to the kitchen and get as much food into me as possible, no matter what it was. Once, it was a bunch of chocolate éclairs. That part wasn't so bad.

My house became another prison. It was spacious and roomy and yet I felt closed in, only seeing the same walls every day. Nobody called or visited. Some afternoons I would lie on my bed and stare out the window at the mountains. There was a whole other world out there: I could *see* it, but I wasn't a part of it. It was untouchable. I was a prisoner to my body and to the house that felt intent of holding me hostage within its walls.

I kept reminding myself that the pregnancy was temporary and soon I'd have a happy, bouncy baby. Yet I worried about what would happen when she arrived. Could I protect her? Would she die like our other son? I'd fight tooth and nail to protect either one of my babies but I felt so weak and drained all the time. I worried that I wouldn't be able to battle if and when the time came.

At twenty-two weeks I had a partial abruption and the hospital told me there was a good chance my daughter would be born that night and that, if she was, she wouldn't live. I spent the whole night trying to think of how I could make her time here meaningful, even if she only lived an hour. I made a list of the songs I could sing to her, the stories I could tell. A nurse brought me a blanket and told me I could bathe her and wrap her in it. "You never know," she shrugged. "She might be a fighter."

She held on.

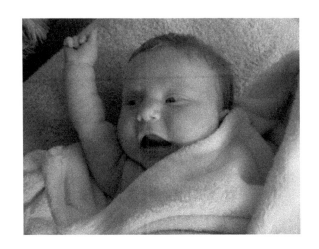

SAM

**So far, Sam had been exempt from most of the
"bad things" that** happened in the house.

Although Pete and I were depressed and never felt as
though we were in top form, especially since James died,
we tried not to let it show in front of Sam. When I felt up to
it, we did as much with him as we could. When I didn't feel
up to it, Pete did it alone. Sam still attended friends'
birthday parties, had picnics, played with his trains, had a
great birthday party (even though hardly anyone we invited
showed up), and we went all out on the major holidays.

His life changed very little. We made sure of that.

Even when I was stuck in bed I would try to watch
cartoons with him, color with him, and tell him stories.

I had failed to save James from his death– a death
everyone swore wasn't my fault. I never *really* assumed
Sam was in any danger, however. At least not for awhile.
We watched over him like a hawk. I didn't even let him eat
grapes or meat anymore for fear of him choking. There was
no longer a fear of him darting out into the road but I
constantly checked on him after he went to bed and I
checked his car seat and seatbelt multiple times.

I was *damned* if I was going to lose another child.

If anything, losing James made me feel even closer to Sam. I clung to him at times, carried away by his sweetness and innocence. Sometimes, I'd sit on the back deck and watch him play with his little cars and I'd cry, thinking how sweet he was and how lucky I was to have him. He, my husband, and I grew stronger together. We were a unit and rarely without one another. We felt safer together. For months after James died I'd wake up in the middle of the night, Pete's hand on my chest to make sure I was breathing. I'd do the same to Sam. It became habit.

But I couldn't always watch him.

Back home from one of my hospital stays I was in bed one night with Pete when some noise only perceptible in sleep woke me up. It was the lightest of sounds, a mere rustling, but I was wide awake within seconds.

The night sky was cloudy so the room was dark. I could barely see my hand in front of my face. Still, there before me, a mysterious object hovered in the air. It appeared to be a small ball of light, bright and translucent.

It hovered mysteriously in the middle of the room, not on one of the walls like a reflection would be. I watched in sheer fascination, not understanding what I was seeing, as it darted away from me and bounced around the room like it was in a pin ball machine.

I wasn't scared at first because the spectacle was just too fascinating. In the beginning, I couldn't quite wrap my head around what I was watching. Indeed, it felt as though the vision before me was on a television screen, not truly real.

It was only after its movements continued on for several minutes that I became disturbed. We lived too high on a mountain to pick up any car lights and neither one of us wore anything shiny that would make that big of a light. As I watched the beam, it shuffled about the room, as if looking for something. For a second it would linger on an object, as though searchingly, and then quickly sprint to the next. Finally, it landed on our family portrait. In a slow, deliberate measure it circled the picture and then seemingly intentionally moved inwards and zeroed in on Sam's face, illuminating his little sweet smile. It remained for several seconds then abruptly whizzed out of the room, flashed down the hall, and shot around the corner into Sam's bedroom.

A cry filled the air, his tiny voice filled with terror.

Without having to think twice, I bounded out of bed and flew into Sam's room, all but leaping through the doorway. I gasped when I got there, however, unable to believe what I was seeing.

Like a scene from a horror movie, what appeared to be a thin white mist covered his floor and was clawing its way up his bed towards him. The thick mist was cool and filmy and I felt dirty where it nipped me around the ankles. I slapped at it and my hand came back grimy and cold.

Sam was sitting up in bed, rubbing his eyes. The light was gone.

"Mommy?" he asked. "I had a bad dream. What's that?" He pointed to the ground.

"Someone must have left the window open. Come on," I said, picking him up (what the doctor didn't know wouldn't hurt either one of us) and leaving his room. I took him to our bed.

He fell right back asleep but I stayed awake the rest of the night. It was impossible to find any kind of peace after that. Every little movement made me jump and I laid on my back, facing the entire room, waiting for a sight of the light which I was certain would return. The rest of the night went by without incident, however.

The next day I did some research on the computer and tried to find an explanation for what I'd seen. Typing "a small ball of light" into Google didn't yield many results. The best I could come up with was either an orb or a willow o' the wisp. Neither one accurately described what I'd seen and the whole willow o' the wisp thing felt too old world for me. I hadn't felt like it wanted me to follow it, although I did get the sense that it knew I was there and was taunting me. The whole incident left me feeling extremely unnerved.

I tried polling some of my friends but soon found, in order to do that, I'd have to explain what happened and I was really tired of always feeling like I had some kind of drama to write or talk about. I didn't want to be the "problem child" anymore. People were tired of hearing about my dead kid, my dead mother-in-law, my awful pregnancies, my dead dogs, my parents' health, and my husband's job loss. Hell, three people I thought I was close to had blocked me on Facebook. The last thing I needed to be talking about was my haunted house now. Instead, I deleted that post and shared a video of a dancing kitten.

A few nights later I turned over in the middle of the night and placed my hand on Sam's chest. Both Pete and I had started doing this to one another, even in our sleep, to check and make sure everyone was still breathing. We were terrified of losing someone else. Nobody felt safe. Usually, we'd feel the steady rise of breath, be satisfied, and drift back to sleep. This time, though, Sam's chest wasn't moving. I woke up with a start and felt his cheek. It was ice cold. "Sam!" I whispered. "Sam!"

My voice caused Pete to wake up and when he saw what I was doing he also placed his hand on Pete's chest. "Sam!" he shouted. The look of panic on his face matched the feeling I had inside. In distress, I curled up in a ball on the edge of the bed and began whimpering.

When Sam didn't answer, Pete lifted him up in the air in his arms and gently shook him. "Sam, wake up!" I could hear the terror in his voice as it cracked. "Sam!"

At last, Sam gasped for breath and started coughing. "Daddy?" he asked sweetly before resting his head on Pete's shoulder and falling back asleep.

Neither I, nor Pete, could go back to sleep.

A week later, it happened again. This time Sam was sleeping with my mother and she was the one to call out to him in a panic, flip the bedroom light on, and try to rouse him. When she told us about it the next day, she did so in tears. "I didn't think he was going to wake up," she moaned. "He was so still and cold."

An appointment to the ENT told us that Sam had developed obstructive sleep apnea and would more than likely need his tonsils removed and that he was, indeed, ceasing to breathe for moments of time in his sleep.

"It's not really dangerous right now," the doctor assured us, "but you'll want to have it taken care of as soon as possible. He's probably not sleeping well and that can make him tired during the day."

When we left the office I turned to Pete. "I don't know that I want to schedule the surgery," I admitted.

"Yeah, I know what you mean," Pete agreed. "I know it's not that dangerous but here lately it seems that if something bad COULD happen, it does happen to us."

We didn't put Sam back in his own bed after that. We kept him with us, in the middle. We were still grieving, of course, and just felt better having him nearby. I slept with either his arms around me or his bony knees poking me in my back. It felt safer having him nearby and I slept more soundly knowing he wasn't down the hall, alone.

One night, though, he woke me up.

"Mommy?" he asked. "Who's that bad man over there? I don't like him standing over there by the window."

It took me a moment to gain my bearings but when I opened my eyes I could see that he was pointing to the corner of the room, next to the doors that led out to the balcony. I couldn't see anything there, not even a shadow. It was very dark.

"What man, baby?" I asked him, peering into the room.

"That man," he insisted. "That bad guy. He's looking at me."

I looked at Sam. His eyes were wide open and he didn't appear to be asleep. Sam wasn't one for sleep walking or talking in his sleep. And besides, his voice was casual and conversation-like. He didn't even sound that afraid, just curious.

"I don't see anyone. What does he look like?"

"I don't know," he shrugged.

"Is he tall or short? Does he have blond hair or black hair?"

"Well," Sam said thoughtfully, "he looks a little bit like me."

I'm not sure why, but that sent chills down my spine. What the hell was he *seeing*?

Leaning over Sam, I shook Pete awake. "Pete, wake up," I hissed. "Sam is sure he sees someone in the room."

"Wha–" Pete mumbled sleepily.

"I can't see anyone but Sam says he's there," I said.

"He's still there," Sam agreed.

Once Pete got awake, Sam repeated to him what he'd said to me. Pete got up, turned the light on, and looked around. There wasn't anything out of the ordinary in the room. I assured Sam that it must have been either a bad dream or a shadow and that nothing could hurt him in the house. We all went back to sleep, although not easily.

The next morning, I asked Sam to show me again where the man had been. I was sure he wouldn't remember the episode. He took me the same spot, however, and was certain he hadn't been dreaming it.

THE ENDING

With everything else that had gone on, we were still looking forward to the arrival of our new daughter and she would be with us in two months, just as long as she lasted through everything that was going on in the pregnancy. In my borrowed wheelchair I was going to do a bit of nursery shopping one afternoon (I hadn't done anything during that pregnancy, maybe partly in fear of what happened in the last one) but as we started out of the house we found we couldn't leave.

All the doors were blocked by thousands of wasps. They'd come overnight. Never in my life had I seen so many wasps. They swarmed each entrance and exit to the house: all the doors and windows, including the balconies, were impassable. There was no way to get out. At one point, to look outside was to see blackness. Not only were they a terrifying sight, the sound of them throwing their winged bodies against the glass panes was unsettling. In my office it was particularly loud and I had to turn the music on to drown them out. It sounded like they were trying to tear down the doors and windows.

Some had even found their way inside to Sam's room and were crawling on his bed. We spent an afternoon just running through the house, killing wasps as they dive-bombed us and Sam cowered on the couch, pointing them out to us like a lieutenant.

We called George and asked him to come over, but his little cans of wasp spray were of little use. Besides, he couldn't find any nests. He and Pete just ended up spraying at them aimlessly, which did little good. We were stuck.

For almost a week we stayed inside the house, only able to venture out after dark when they went to sleep.

And then, one day, they were gone. Just as quickly as they showed up, they disappeared.

Pete and I finally ordered the nursery furniture for the bedroom, we couldn't use James', and I started shopping online for bedding. We talked about what color we would paint her room.

I hadn't packed up any of James' clothes or toys yet. I knew I had to, but it was hard. Some days I couldn't even bring myself to go in there. We kept the door closed most of the time. Little by little, though, I was getting used to the idea of putting his things away and trying to store them. We talked about moving his nursery decorations into our office so that we could still leave them out as a way for

James to continue to have a "room" in our house. I liked that idea.

And then, just one month before my due date, and a day after being released from the hospital for the umpteenth time, we received a phone call: The owner of the house was returning; we had to move out.

Moving was a bittersweet time for us. On the one hand, I felt deep inside me that there was something terribly wrong within the house. A primal urge wanted us GONE. Yet...I felt connected to it.

For me, my James was still within those walls somewhere. He wasn't in a Heaven or buried in the ground. He was more than just in my heart. He was still there. The thought of leaving him terrified me. Nobody could tell me I carried him within my heart. Occasionally, I still heard his little cries within those rooms. Sometimes, when I couldn't sleep, I slept in a sleeping bag in his nursery. I hadn't even completely packed up his room yet. Now, I was forced to do it with speed. I locked myself in there, night after night, boxing up clothing and crying over little hats and blankets and outfits—some he'd never been able to use. He still had a clothes hamper full of dirty clothes. I hadn't been able to wash them. They were still covered in spit up and milk. I couldn't wash them now. Instead, I placed them in Ziploc bags and buried them in a trunk, along with the other clothes he'd worn in his brief life.

I felt cheated, disillusioned. So much had been taken from us within those walls. We'd lost so much. Not only had we lost our son, we'd lost our innocence. Never again would we be able to believe that things always worked out for the best, that things always happened for a reason, or that everything eventually works out in the end. We were shattered. We'd lost our child, friends, and sometimes it felt like our minds. And now the house was just spitting us out as though finished with us. It didn't need us anymore. It had taken everything it possibly could.

Many people might think we would be glad to get away, glad to go someplace where we'd have better luck and could start anew. We weren't yet thinking of our time there in this manner, however. It was our home. It had become my cocoon. I was as wrapped up in it as though I was a spider caught in a sticky, messy web high up in a tree. I'd spent almost a year and a half of illness there.

Most of our friends were gone. It was difficult for me to remember what it was like to get out, socialize, and enjoy time away from the house. It had been so long since I had done that. I hated being shut up in it, but I was almost dependent upon it as well. Leaving that mountaintop was frightening. I almost felt as though I no longer knew the world; I felt as though I had been living within a vortex.

So what happened when we moved? It's at this point in the story when things could go one of two ways: They could either get better or not change.

In many ways, they got better.

The rest of the pregnancy, for instance, was fine. We found another house and while the complications continued, they didn't worsen. Lily (not her real name) was born on time and healthy. On the other hand, within the first two weeks of her life she suffered terrible seizures and had to be hospitalized. Her newborn screening came back with a problem: she tested for a rare genetic disorder that no other child in the state had; if not treated properly it would cause mental retardation and eventually death. At the age of three, though, you'd never know it and she's healthy as a horse.

Yet, once we moved out of the house, Sam's sleep apnea improved.

Nobody else close to us has died.

We did discover, however, that many of the headaches and other issues I had there in the house were the result of a medical problem and I ended up needing brain surgery a year later.

That came out of the blue.

Even moving presented its own set of unique problems. When I arrived at the business to pick up our U-Haul we'd ordered for the next several days, I discovered it had been given away. Our movers never showed up and we frantically had to rush about and locate people who would move our belongings for us. We ended up finding total strangers who lived nearby to do it.

Oh, and while a friend was helping us pack to move? She found several scorpions, just kind of hanging out in our bathrooms and kitchen. They were in our clothes hampers, in our pots and pans, and scurrying through our cabinets.

NOW

So now, with time and distance between us, do I feel like there was something paranormal going on within the house? Maybe. I'm now able to look back on our time there with a critical eye and wonder. Perhaps we experienced a string of bad luck in those two years. It happens to everyone, right? And the noises, bumps in the night, and things we thought we saw? Maybe they were nothing.

Other times, I'm not so sure.

I watch the paranormal shows on television and our story doesn't compare. And yet, I think about the light bouncing in our room and darting into Sam's and I wonder.

I still think of the beauty of the house and wish I could live in a large, open place like that again. On the other hand, I've been unable to drive past the road leading to it for almost three years now because the very thought of doing so makes me sick to my stomach.

Our story isn't anything like the Hollywood films would have you believe and sometimes I talk myself out of it. I begin thinking that it really was just a string of coincidences...but then I remember the singing in the night, the banging around during the day, the random deaths...

Sometimes, I think there might have been an energy force there, and whatever that was there acted like a catalyst. If there was something even a little bit wrong, it could take that and twist it and compound it to make it greater. It fed off things.

It created a perfect storm.

Long after we moved we discovered the former residents lost a baby in the house as well. It happened in the very room James died in. On James' birthday.

I have no answers. The cars were going to quit eventually, wasps come out in the spring, pregnancies can be bad, nobody knows why some infants mysteriously die in their sleep, dogs can die of Parvo and other diseases, the wind can open doors, fog can get inside homes...

But I keep my eyes open, I watch my children closely, and I pay attention. Because sometimes, especially late at night, I still feel as though that other shoe might just drop again.

AFTERWORD

When *The Maple House* was first released, I did it under my pen name for several reasons. I still live in the same town where the story took place and I didn't want to bring too much attention to the house, for both personal and legal reasons.

The biggest reason, however, was because the story IS so deeply personal. I knew that reviewers would pick the story apart, some claiming it wasn't "scary enough" and others even questioning its validity. Since it pertains to the death of my son I didn't know if I could handle the criticisms or even the negative emails I sometimes get. A popular true haunting show on cable even contacted us and expressed interest in filming an episode based on the occurrences. In the end, however, we weren't sure we wanted to see our lives acted out on the screen for entertainment purposes.

The fact is, the story is true and while it might not be as scary as many stories you see on the various television programs and "based on true events" movies, it was scary to us. Most hauntings revolve around the mundane, the everyday life occurrences. They're small and grow progressively more active, almost before you're aware of them. I am still not sure if what we experienced in The

Maple House was an actual haunting, but I can say that my family feels much better now that we are out of there.

I was recently on a podcast and the interviewer asked me if I knew I was a "sensitive." I reckon I must be a little. I can't communicate with spirits or beckon them, but there have been several times in my life in which they seem to have found me. Did the house in Mount Sterling start that, or was it even earlier? I don't know.

I have not been visited by the spirit of my son since he died. Two years after his death, however, on the anniversary, his funeral lilies bloomed in the middle of the night. It was the first time they had blossomed since the funeral.

Like what you read? A review for an author is like a tip–we depend on them! Please visit

http://www.amazon.com/Maple-House-Story-Haunting-Hauntings-ebook/dp/B00KYLKFCS/

And choose "write a customer review" if you enjoyed *The Maple House.*

ABOUT THE AUTHOR

Jeanie Dyer is a pen name for author:

Rebecca Patrick-Howard

Rebecca originally wrote THE MAPLE HOUSE under a pseudonym to protect the family's privacy. Rebecca is the author of several books including the paranormal mystery series, Taryn's Camera. She lives in eastern Kentucky with her husband and two living children.

For updates, free books (audio and digital books), sign up for Rebecca's VIP mailing list. She promises not to spam you!

www.rebeccaphoward.net

Rebecca's other books include:

Taryn's Camera Series

Windwood Farm (Book 1)

Griffith Tavern (Book 2)

Dark Hollow Road (Book 3)

Shaker Town (Book 4)

Jekyll Island (Book 5-Coming October 2015)

True Hauntings

Four Months of Terror

A Summer of Fear

The Maple House

Two Weeks (Coming September 2015)

Three True Tales of Terror

Haunted Estill County

More Tales from Haunted Estill County

Other Books

Coping with Grief: The Anti-Guide to Infant Loss

Three Minus Zero

Estill County in Photos

Finding Henry: A Journey Into Eastern Europe

Haunted: Ghost Children A Collection of Stories from Beyond

Visit her website at www.rebeccaphoward.net to sign up for her newsletter to receive free books, special offers, and news.

TWO WEEKS: A FAMILY'S TRUE HAUNTING EXCERPT

She needed to get out of the tub, she needed to grab her towel, but that would mean turning her head and looking at the door. The thought of what might be there stunned her in fear, the most vivid sensation she'd ever felt. "Daddy," she whimpered, praying he'd be able to hear her thoughts and come to her. She thought of calling out downstairs, bringing up one of her siblings, but her throat was tight. She didn't think she could holler if she tried.

With slow, easy movements she lifted herself from the tub and grabbed the towel on the back of the toilet. The softness felt good on her skin, its weight a shield against whatever was out there. Feeling stronger now she slowly turned to face the door, her eyes clenched shut and her teeth grinding against each other.

With determined resolution she gathered all the courage she'd ever had, thinking about the super heroes in movies she loved, and opened her eyes to what was waiting for her.

The figure that stood before her was just a few feet away. If they'd both stretched out their hands they could've touched one another. The long hair, dark dress that brushed the floor and delicate hands could only belong to a woman. Where her face should've been, however, there was nothing but a pale void.

"Ahhhhkkkkk!!!!" Laura screamed, her voice returning in a ferocious roar. "Dad-EE!"

The figure gave out a solitary hiss, like a balloon running out of air, and disappeared.

Laura was still standing wet in the middle of the bathroom floor when Jimmy and Jenny found her. Shaking and crying, they led her to her bedroom where Jenny petted on her and helped her dress. Jimmy marched up and down the hallway, checking closets, looking under beds, and making sure all the windows were locked.

There was no question about whether or not they believed Laura. They both knew now, for sure, that their new house was haunted.

Available on Amazon
http://www.amazon.com/Two-Weeks-True-Haunting-Hauntings-ebook/dp/B013USPH1A/

Milton Keynes UK
Ingram Content Group UK Ltd.
UKHW021440090224
437562UK00010B/991